MY FIRST
Yoga Class

By Alyssa Satin Capucilli

Photographs by Jill Wachter

Ready-to-Read

Simon Spotlight

New York London Toronto Sydney New Delhi

For Laura and Kate, my favorite yogis

—A. S. C.

Dedicated to all the little bodies on the

journey of finding peace within

—J. W.

SIMON SPOTLIGHT
An imprint of Simon & Schuster Children's Publishing Division
1230 Avenue of the Americas, New York, New York 10020
This Simon Spotlight edition August 2017
Text copyright © 2017 by Alyssa Satin Capucilli
Photographs and illustrations copyright © 2017 by Simon & Schuster, Inc.
For information about special discounts for bulk purchases, please contact Simon & Schuster Special Sales at
1-866-506-1949 or business@simonandschuster.com.
Manufactured in the United States of America 0518 LAK
2 4 6 8 10 9 7 5 3
Library of Congress Cataloging-in-Publication Data
Names: Capucilli, Alyssa Satin, 1957– author. | Wachter, Jill, illustrator.
Title: My first yoga class / by Alyssa Satin Capucilli ; photographs by Jill Wachter.
Description: Simon Spotlight hardcover/paperback edition. | New York : Simon Spotlight, 2017.
Series: Ready-to-read | Audience: Age 3–5.
Identifiers: LCCN 2017025851| ISBN 9781534404847 (paperback) | ISBN 9781534404854 (hardcover)
ISBN 9781534404861 (eBook)
Subjects: LCSH: Hatha yoga—Juvenile literature. | Exercise—Juvenile literature. | BISAC: JUVENILE NONFICTION
/ Readers / Beginner. | JUVENILE NONFICTION / Sports & Recreation / General. | JUVENILE NONFICTION / Social
Issues / New Experience.
Classification: LCC RA781.7 .C3572 2017 | DDC 613.7/046—dc23
LC record available at https://lccn.loc.gov/2017025851
ISBN 978-1- 5344-0485-4 (hc)
ISBN 978-1-5344-0484-7 (pbk)
ISBN 978-1-5344-0486-1 (eBook)

Today is my very first yoga class!

I have comfy clothes
and water, too.

First we pick a yoga mat.

I choose light blue!

It is time for yoga class
to start.

Soft, gentle music fills the room.

I feel calm and relaxed
as I breathe in and out.

My tummy fills with air
like a balloon!

I sit on my mat as
quiet as a mouse.
I take a deep breath in.

When I breathe out,

I roar like a lion. **ROAR!**

Then I do it again!

Like a small furry cat,

I perch on all fours.

I curve my back so round.

Meow, meow, meow, purr!

We can make cat sounds!

Calling all dogs!
Calling all pups!

Our paws press down,
but our wagging tails go up!

My butterfly wings
flutter in the breeze!

I pretend I can fly

high up to the trees!

I balance like a flamingo
in a lake.

I stretch and hiss
just like a snake!

Then we lay like starfish,
as still as can be.

What will we be next time?

I can't wait to see!

Do you want to try yoga?

Don't forget to find a grown-up to help you read and learn about the yoga poses in this book!

Mice, Lions, Cats, and Dogs!

1 Mouse

Sit as quietly as a mouse.

Take a deep breath in through your nose. . . .

Breathe out softly through your mouth.

You can curl up like a mouse too!

Sit on your heels. Lower your head to the floor.

This is also known as Child's Pose.

2 Lion

Sit with your bottom between
your knees.
Take a deep breath in. . . .
Now breathe out and **ROAR!**

Stick your lion tongue
out too!

ROARRR!

3 Cat

Kneel on all four paws!
Breathe out and round
your back like a kitty
stretching in the sun!
Meow, meow, purr!

4 Down Dog

Kneel on your paws and curl
your toes under.
Push your front paws down and
lift your tail up!

Ruff! Stretch like a puppy!

Butterflies, Trees, Flamingos, and More!

1 Butterfly

Can you move your knees up and down
like a butterfly fluttering its wings?
Remember to wiggle your antennae too!
Where will your butterfly fly?

2 Tree

Stand up tall and feel your roots
stretch into the ground.

Can you bring one foot up?

Can you reach your branches up to the sky?

3 Flamingo

Balance on one leg like a flamingo.

You can use your flamingo wings to help you!

4 Snake

Lie flat with your hands by your shoulders.

Take a deep breath in. Breathe out and Hissss!

Slide your chest and head forward and off the floor.

Hissss!

Hissss! You're a slithering snake!

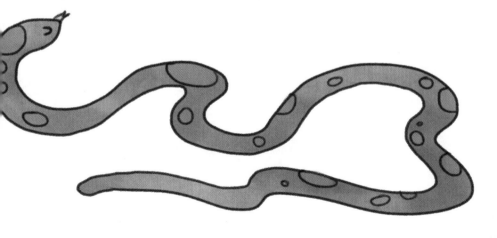

Relaxation Time!

Lie on your back or tummy
like a starfish in the sand
or a rag doll.
You've worked hard and had fun—
now it is time to breathe and rest!

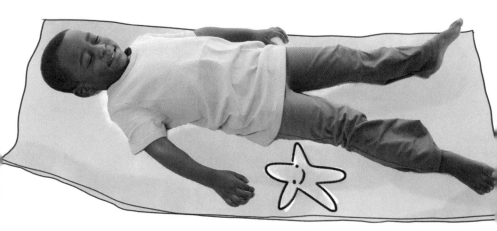

Yoga is . . . the best!